Crayola®

Ultimate Sticker and Activity Book

BuzzPop

Hello!

Connect the dots to see who is waving to you.

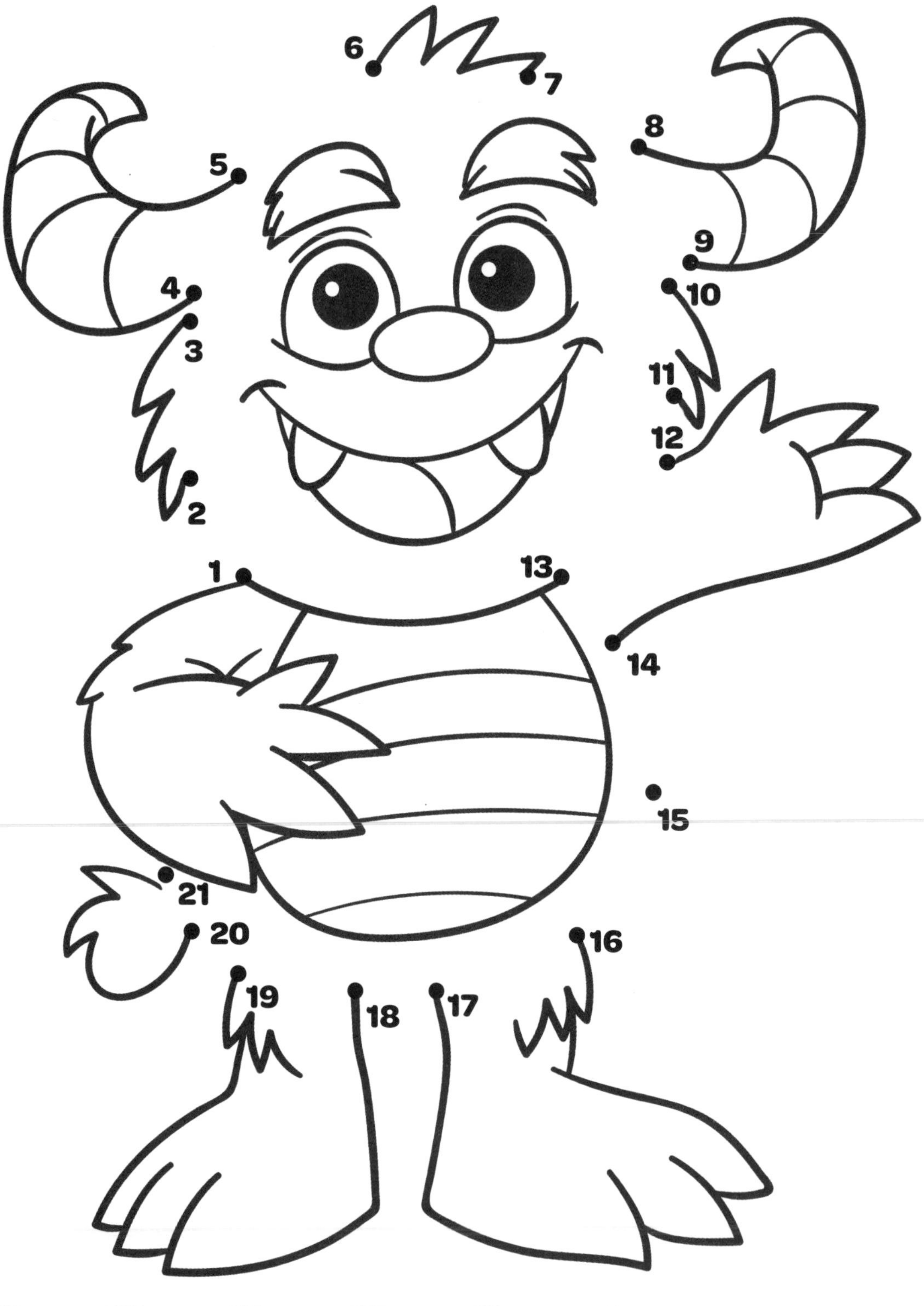

Answers on page 61

Colorful Rows

Crayons come in so many colors.
Find the sticker for the one that comes
next in each row.

1

2

3

Answers on page 61

Magical Changes

This fairy can magically change her appearance. Can you circle the 5 differences between the images?

Answers on page 61

Royal Fashion

A yellow dress with silver sparkles, please!

Feeling Fancy

What does a princess wear in the summertime? Circle the objects to make your princess the best dressed!

Answers on page 61

Name That Animal!

Draw a line to match each animal to its name.

Turtle

Lion

Bat

Answers on page 61

What's Hatching?

How many eggs are in the nest?

Your answer:

Answers on page 61

Welcome to the Farm

The farm is a busy place.
Put farm stickers in this space.

Farm Friends

Put a circle around each farm animal that is brown. How many did you find?

Your answer:

Answers on page 61

Who Says "Cock-a-Doodle-Doo"?

Connect the dots to find out. Then color the picture.

Answers on page 61

Back to the Barn

The cow had a nice day out in the field. Now it's time to go back to the barn. Help her get there.

Answers on page 62

Fantasy Under the Sea

Can you decorate this castle for a seashell fairy? Color it in and add some stickers!

The Amazing Ocean

Use your stickers to show all the creatures who live in the sea!

A Colorful Fish

Use the guide to finish the picture.

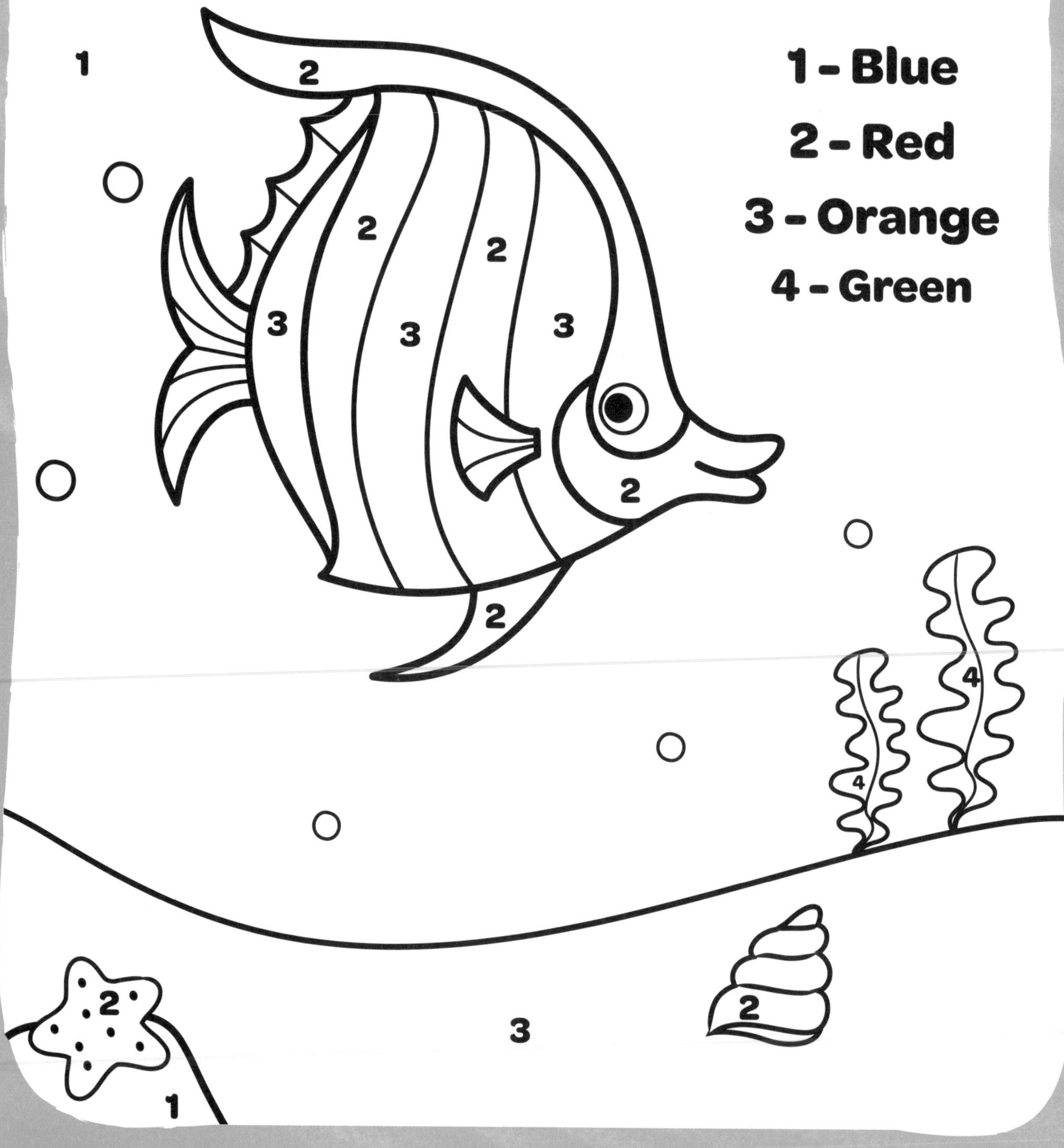

1 - Blue

2 - Red

3 - Orange

4 - Green

Fin to Fin

Which path will get the fish to his friend?

Your answer:

Answers on page 62

Swimming in the Sea

Draw a line to match each animal that lives in the ocean to its name.

Seahorse

Crab

Fish

Answers on page 62

Underwater Adventure

Draw some interesting sea creatures for this scuba diver to discover.

Blue Bubbles

How many bubbles are there?

Your answer:

Answers on page 62

Ahoy, Mateys!

Use your stickers to complete the picture of this fishy pirate!

Answers on page 62

Here in the Jungle

Trees and grass make a jungle green.
Jungle animals will complete the scene.
Add your jungle animal stickers here!

I Spy Butterflies!

Follow the flowers to get this zebra to the butterflies.

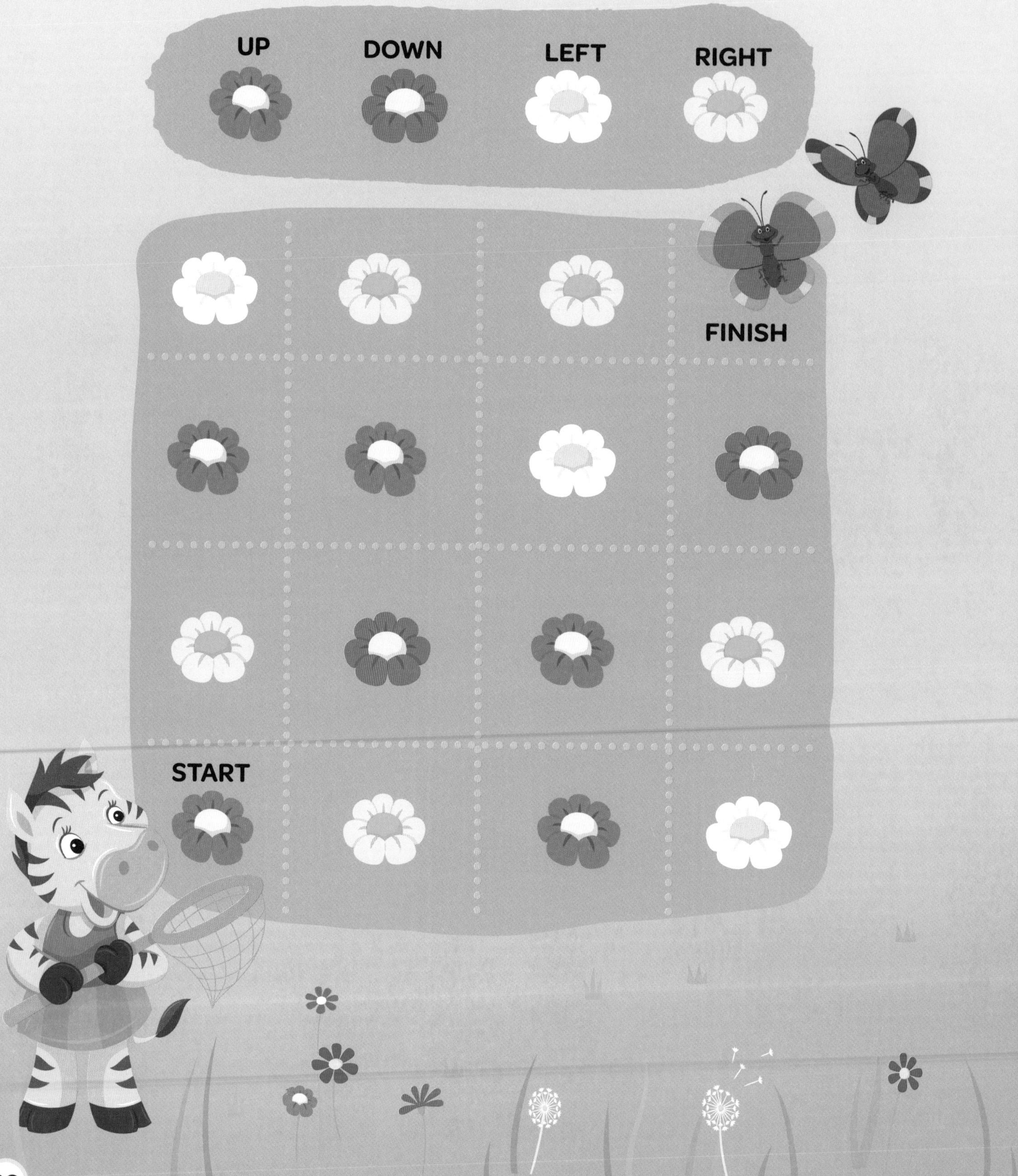

Answers on page 62

Three Jungle Critters

Each of these animals should appear once in each row and column. Use stickers to fill the empty squares.

Answers on page 62

A Cat of Many Colors

Can you make each of this tiger's stripes a different color?

Weight Lifting Champ

No one can lift more weight than this gorilla can!
Give him a trophy sticker for his strength.
Draw some bananas for him, too.

Look at Me!

Most parrots have very bright colors. Color this one in as many bright colors as you can.

It's a Jungle in Here

Find and circle these animals' names in the puzzle below.

HIPPO SNAKE ZEBRA RHINO

H	W	J	O	M	P	O
Q	I	W	L	O	I	Z
L	S	P	Q	N	Z	E
V	I	F	P	I	U	B
L	X	Y	L	O	Q	R
V	S	N	A	K	E	A
I	R	H	I	N	O	G

Answers on page 63

What's for Lunch?

In the thought balloon above his head, draw what the elephant is thinking of eating for lunch.

Design a Zebra

Most zebras have stripes. But this one can have any pattern and be any colors you like!

Hanging Around

What colors do you think this snake curled up on this branch should be? You decide!

Bike Riders

Get the hedgehog bike rider to his friend so they can ride together!

Answers on page 63

Out in the Yard

Fill in this scene with your backyard animal stickers!

Backyard Visitors

Find and circle the names of these animals that might be in your backyard.

CAT BIRD BEE SKUNK SNAIL

Y	T	U	I	S	B
C	A	T	Z	K	E
B	I	R	D	U	E
M	I	S	P	N	U
X	O	Y	L	K	Q
S	N	A	I	L	P

Answers on page 63

Go Fetch!

Get this dog to his ball!

Answers on page 63

Squeak, Squeak . . .

Find and circle the mouse that is different from the others.

Answers on page 63

Garden Playground

A backyard garden is a great place to play! Color in this fun scene!

Ribbit, Ribbit!

Copy this friendly frog's smiling face into the empty grid on the next page, square by square. Then color both froggy faces.

In the Forest

A forest has a lot of trees.
Add some stickers as you please!

We Love Camping!

Color this cozy camp scene and add some buggy stickers.

Count the Candles!

How many candles are on the cake?
Count them up and write the number.
Remember to make a wish!

Your answer:

Answers on page 63

Rabbits Love Carrots

Can you circle the 5 differences between these two scenes?

Answers on page 63

Who Says "Meow"?

Connect the dots and see! Then color the picture.

Answers on page 64

My Favorite Animal

Draw a picture of your favorite animal in the picture frame.

Fluttering Butterflies

Find the two butterflies that are the same and color them. Then color all the other butterflies different colors! How many butterflies are there in all?

Your answer: ______

Answers on page 64

Count the Bees, Please

How many bees do you see buzzing around?

Your answer:

Answers on page 64

Pretty Birdie

Use the guide to finish the picture.

1 - Blue

2 - Orange

3 - Brown

4 - Green

In His Paws

What is the puppy holding in his paws? Write down the first letter and then every second letter in the circle to find out.

Answers on page 64

Which Way to Earth?

Which path will get this space traveler to planet Earth?

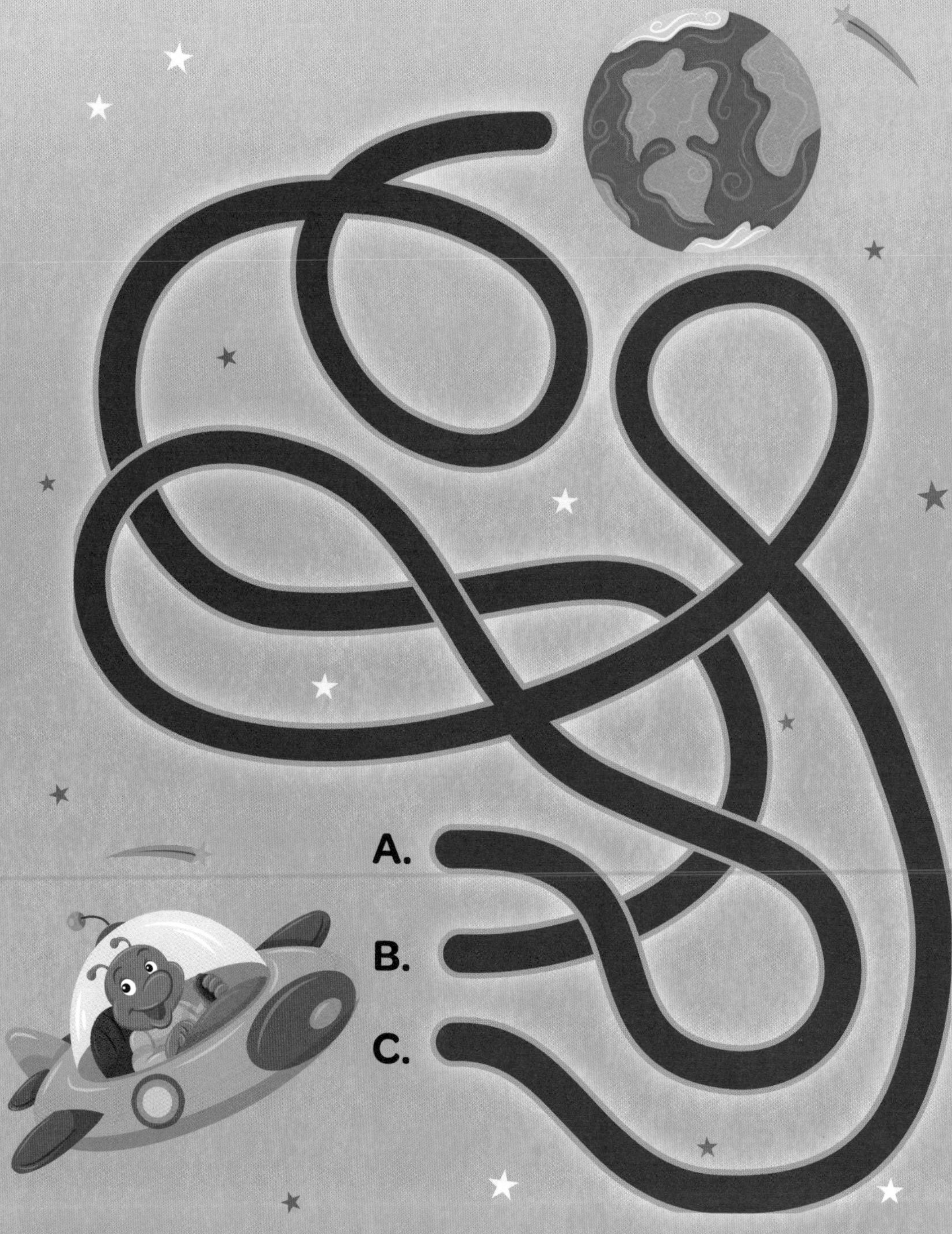

Answers on page 64

Out-of-This-World Mail!

Pretend you are an astronaut and write a postcard to your best friend on Earth. Describe what you are seeing. Then, add a sticker stamp.

Now You Know the Wonderful World

Give yourself a reward sticker in the spaces below next to each scene you've completed

Farm

Yard

Ocean

Forest

Jungle

Ask an adult to help you cut out this cool poster! Add stickers and hang it on your door or wall.

Answers

Page 2

Page 3

Pages 4-5

Page 7

Page 8

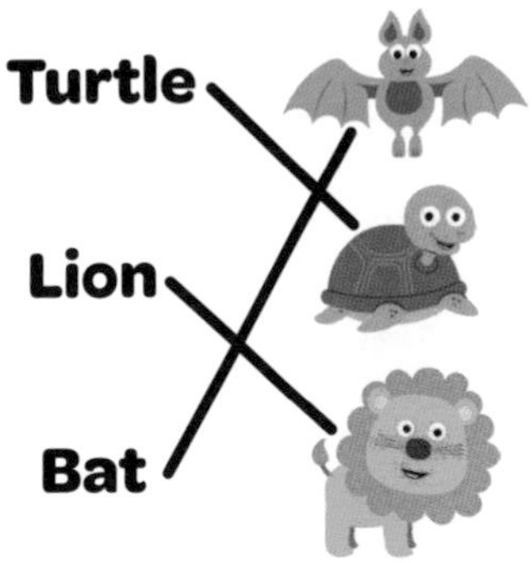

Page 9

4 eggs

Page 12

Page 13

Page 14

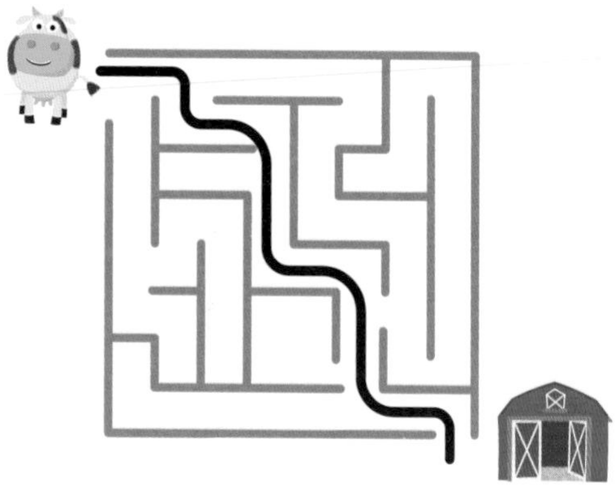

Page 19

Page 20

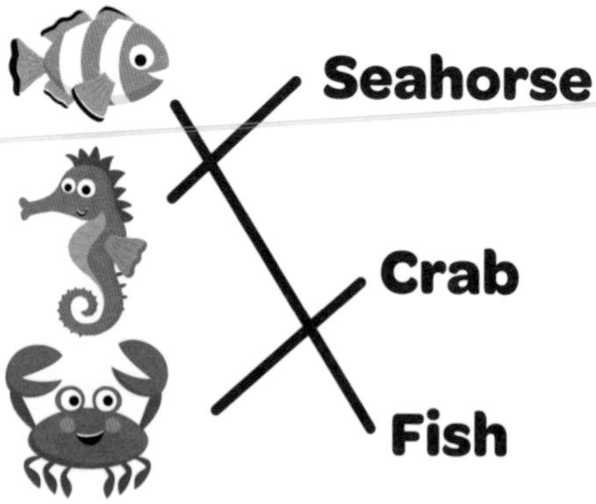

Page 22

There are 7 bubbles

Page 23

Page 26

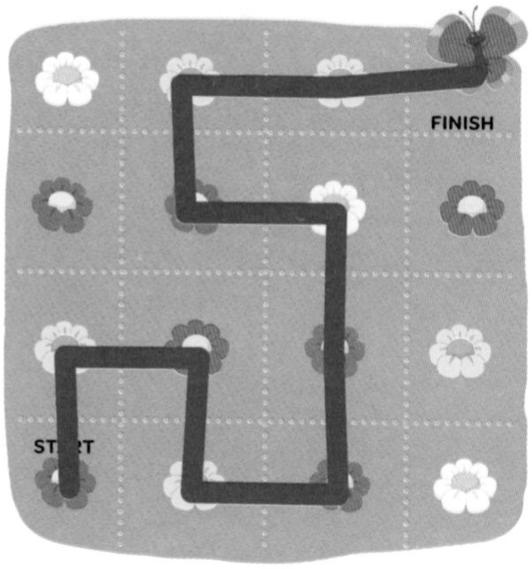

Page 27

Page 31

H	W	J	O	M	P	O
Q	I	W	L	O	I	Z
L	S	P	Q	N	Z	E
V	I	F	P	I	U	B
L	X	Y	L	O	Q	R
V	S	N	A	K	E	A
I	R	H	I	N	O	G

Page 35

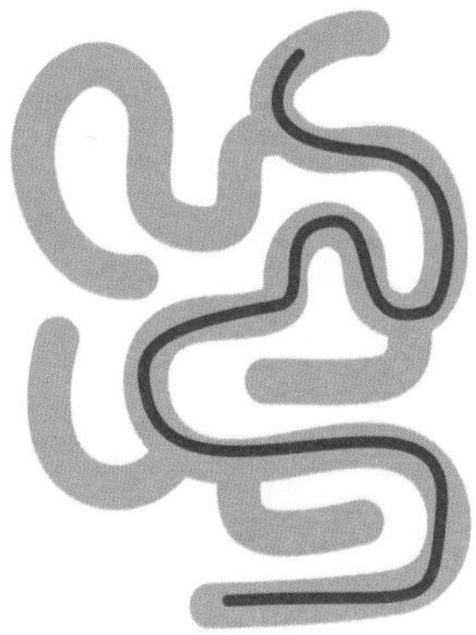

Page 38

Y	T	U	I	S	B
C	A	T	Z	K	E
B	I	R	D	U	E
M	I	S	P	N	U
X	O	Y	L	K	Q
S	N	A	I	L	P

Page 39

Page 40

Page 47

There are 5 candles

Pages 48-49

Page 50

Page 52

There are 5 butterflies

Page 53

There are 4 bees

Page 55

SNOWBALL

Page 56

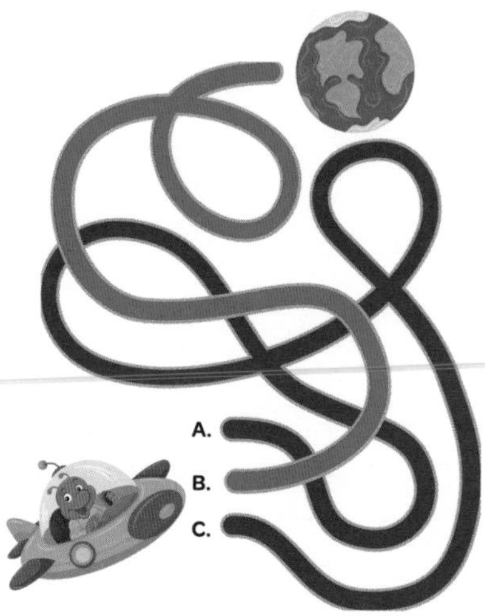